INCREDIBLE 420
EDIBLES

Fabulous Recipes for Baking with Marijuana

By S. Jackson

ISBN: 9781983261510

To my spouse, always.

Disclaimer/Common Sense Warning

This book is intended for adults over the age of 21. Marijuana is a controlled substance that is strictly regulated in North America and throughout the world. The author does not advocate or encourage anyone to break the law. Information contained in this cookbook is presented for education, entertainment and information only. The author will not be held liable for any damage or injury that results from the use of the information within this book.

The ideas, methods, procedures and suggestions contained in this cookbook are not intended as a substitute for consulting with your physician. The recipes contained within this cookbook have been created for the techniques and ingredients indicated. The author is not responsible for your specific health or allergy needs that may require supervision, medical or otherwise. Nor is the author responsible for any adverse reactions you may have to the recipes contained within this cookbook, whether you follow them as written, or modify to suit your personal dietary needs or tastes.

Cannabis-infused foods should <u>never</u> be given to children or those under 21 years of age.

CONTENTS

Contents

Hello and Welcome!

like recipes that don't suck.

We're past the time when if you wanted Edibles, you dumped a bunch of brick pot in a box of brownie mix and hoped for the best, and just got crunchy weedy brownies instead. Worst of all, they really didn't do the trick.

This cookbook is for those who want more from their Edibles. Having a dinner party? Want to wow your guests with dessert, the crowning finale of your meal? Or maybe you are a caretaker of someone who is ill and uses medical marijuana and wants high quality baked goods. Perhaps it is you who are tired of substandard Edibles and you want to treat yourself with treats (ha!).

This is for you.

My Why – Medical Marijuana Edibles

At a difficult time in my life, I would come home from work and stress-bake. The best part of my day was coming home, making a new recipe and firing up my oven.

A suggestion from my spouse turned into a reality – just go to culinary school. And so, I did. I've been a professional pastry chef for fifteen years and certified by the American Culinary Foundation. I've worked as a restaurant pastry chef, in bakeries, delis and cafes, catering and confectionary kitchens as well as teaching culinary school.

Years ago, I had a girlfriend who had an emergency hysterectomy. Her spouse asked if I could make some Edibles to help her manage the pain. She was hell-bent on not using opioids for pain, as they made her very sick and puke her guts out. I didn't know what to do (and this was before marijuana was legal *anywhere*) and there wasn't a lot of information readily available.

Knowing that THC binds to the fat cells in food as the mechanism that carries it into the body to be absorbed by the digestive system was my first clue. More is better, right? So, I steeped a quarter ounce of marijuana (7g) in a small amount of butter for 24 hours, strained it and let it cool. As we were also renting an apartment at the time, it was also a mad scramble to cover up the unmistakable smell of cooking marijuana.

That batch of butter turned out neon green and boy, was it potent! The quick breads I made were green! The cookies! GREEN! But, even though they were potent (and helped my girlfriend immensely), they tasted weedy and grassy. For the next batch of butter, I promised to do better.

I've refined my process and harnessed a series of recipes that will either highlight the flavor of marijuana or cover it up – whatever you're looking for at the time.

I've seen firsthand the effect that medical marijuana has on people suffering in pain. It is a delight that now there are 29 states in the USA (and now Canada legalizing!) that allow you to get a prescription. However, in many of those states, it is very highly regulated and rather difficult to get a prescription and the conditions of eligibility may not cover your particular ailment. Further refining of legislation is obviously needed.

Dosing – Or, How Not to Lose a Day of Your Life

E dibles work differently than smoking, as they must be absorbed through the digestive system rather than smoke via the lungs. Depending on the strain you use (Sativa, Indica, Hybrid or just CBD) determines what effect it will have on you.

Start with an empty stomach and at the lowest dose and **wait** at least 2 hours to see how the Edible will affect you. As they say, Start Low, Go High. As a rule:

> Sativa will usually make you happy, energized and uplifted
> Indica will usually make you more calm, relaxed, better body high, muscle relaxant
> Hybrids come in different ratios (60/40 etc.) and follow the traits of the dominant strain
> CBD (Cannabidiol) is not psychoactive and is used to treat anxiety and seizure disorders

When I first started making Edibles, I was not aware that you could adjust your "speed". Everything I made was very strong and people reported losing a day (one person said she watched the entire schedule of H&G tv, 14 hours' worth). Sometimes, you just need a little lift for a while and not be incapacitated.

Since everyone is different (what is too strong for me may be just right for you) you need to be able to calculate the dosage so that you don't overdo it. Unlike other Schedule 1 drugs, you cannot overdose on marijuana. You will be really quite uncomfortable and the side effects unpleasant, but you will not kick the bucket.

A word of caution: consuming too many edibles can be rough on the digestive system. Signs you've overdone it: diarrhea, stomach cramping and bloating. That's your cue to ease up a bit, ok?

Dosing is a difficult subject to tackle. Where marijuana is legal, states allow lab testing and quantification of the THC levels as well as strain identification. In states where marijuana is prohibited, without access to lab service to determine THC content, we will have to guesstimate. If you are lucky enough to live in a state where the dispensary has done the math and THC percentage for you, this will be easy.

I have used a dosing calculator based on an average percent of THC found in marijuana, 12%. This average is used for my recipes, giving you an idea of portion size and dose contained within the portion. If you know your THC percentage, please follow the link on the references page and make your own calculations.

The recipes in this book are meant to provide a lower lift so you can get on with your day, not incapacitate you. However, you are welcome to modify according to your needs and desires.

If the approximate dose listed in the recipe seems too high, cut the amount of infused fat in half. For example, Chocolate Chippers are 5mg each cookie and that's too much for you. Instead of baking with all infused Cannabis Butter, use half Cannabis Butter, half plain ol' unsalted butter. That will cut your dosage in half. Conversely, if you know that you require a higher THC dosage, you can make all infusions with more marijuana recommended, but keep the fat measurements the same.

Use marijuana to infuse that has at least 10% THC. This excludes brick pot, schwag, cuttings, trim and shake.

Warnings:

- ➤ **Keep Edibles clearly labeled and away from children under 21 years of age.** I can't emphasize this enough.

- ➤ **Keep your Edibles out of the reach of pets.** Yes, there's a reason I'm telling you this.

- ➤ **Do not bake while high.** Just don't.

- ➤ **Resist the urge to lick the spoons, beaters, etc.** See item above.

- ➤ It is a good idea to have other baked goods available that do not contain marijuana. Stories of people who overdo it are common, because my recipes are really just that good. Let's say you have an Edible and 2 hours later you get the munchies. And you see the loaf of banana bread and have another slice (and it tastes sooooo goooood), only to realize later that you have eaten even more Edibles and it will take you a lot longer to come down (and you had things to do, etc.).

Best Baking Practices

have made *all* these recipes many times and will not lead you astray. Trust that if you follow the directions it will be a-ok. Still unsure? Questions? Email me! My address is found on the About page at the end of the book.

First: Follow my directions. No. Really. If you make things out of the order in which they are presented in the recipe, your baked goods will not turn out and you will be sad. Baking ≠ cooking.

Mise en place. This is a fancy French term that means "Every thing in its place, and a place for every thing". In other words, get your poop in a group <u>before</u> you even start mixing. Measure out all your stuff (just like you see the peeps on the cooking channels do), make sure you have all the necessary ingredients, pans or baking tins and *THEN* start with the mixing/folding/stirring/etc. Trust me. Your baking life will be SO MUCH EASIER! Skeptics prove me wrong here!

Room Temp: make sure your butter, eggs and all ingredients (save dairy, e.g. sour cream/yoghurt) are room temperature before beginning. Yes, it makes a difference.

Use a Timer: Sometimes (who am I kidding, a lot of times) I get distracted and forget I have things in the oven. And then they are arcwelded toast. Ugh. Set a timer for yourself! Use the microwave, use your phone, do an old school windy-up kitchen timer, use something! SET A TIMER. I have an android phone and super love the app called Kitchen Timer that has three different time sets so I can keep track of three separate things. Genius.

Measure Everything Accurately: Dry ingredients (flour, sugar, baking soda, etc.) are to be measured using the "dip and sweep" method. In other words, dip your measuring cup into the bag of flour. Use the back of a knife (or even your finger) and sweep off the top, making the ingredient level with the measuring cup. DO NOT pack the flour down in the measuring cup, or all your baked goods will be really dry and may fall apart.

The only ingredient that gets packed down is brown sugar. To measure brown sugar, you fill the measuring cup halfway, pack down the sugar into the cup and then repeat until the measuring cup is full and level.

Liquids? Use a liquid measuring cup. Don't use a dry measure (regular measuring cups) for a liquid substance. Your recipe will be off, and you will be sad.

When measuring sticky liquids such as molasses or honey, use pan spray in your measuring utensil and your sticky stuff will slide right out. This makes clean-up a snap and ensures an accurate measurement.

When using your scale: turn on the scale and place your mixing bowl on the scale and hit Tare or Zero. This will zero-out your scale and allow you to measure just the ingredient without adding in the weight of the bowl.

Common measurement abbreviations:
tsp = teaspoon
tbsp = tablespoon
c = cup
oz = ounce
lb = pound
g = gram
kg = kilogram

Pool Your Eggs: This means crack your eggs into another container rather than cracking an egg directly into a batter. This is a no-no for many reasons, the first being we do not want egg shells in our baked goods. Number Two is that sometimes we get eggs that are not as fresh or that one weird bloody egg (ish pew). If this happens, then you must throw out your batter, which will make you mad. So, just pool your eggs already!

Parchment Paper: Use this to line cookie sheets and loaf pans, or to cut out circles to line cake pans. It's easily attainable and will make your clean-up a snap! Parchment can also be used more than once for cookies, provided you didn't bake something super messy (Chocolate Crinkles, I'm looking at you).

Wrapping your Goodies: Wait to bag up your baked goods until they are completely cool. Your baked goods continue to release moisture as they cool. If you bag and seal while still warm, you trap in that moisture and it will cause your goodies to mold faster, as well as soften in structure. So, let everything hang out until it is completely cool. Then, cut into portions (when applicable) and then bag and LABEL your treats.

High-Altitude Baking: If you are living 3000 – 8000 feet above sea level, you will need to adjust the recipes contained in this book (tested at sea level).
As a general rule: at 5000 feet (about a mile up)

Reduce leavening by 1/8 tsp to ¼ tsp
Reduce sugar by 1 to 2 tablespoons for each cup in the recipe.
Increase the liquids, adding 2 to 4 tablespoons per each cup
Increase your oven temp by 25 degrees.

For more information, check out the wise sages at King Arthur Baking (link on References page) and if you really want to go down the rabbit hole, Colorado State University Extension school has a great book, entitled "A Complete Guide to High Altitude Baking".

Last   but   MOST   IMPORTANT   --   Decarb   Your   Marijuana:
Decarb, aka decarboxylation is a process that releases the full range of psychoactive compounds found within marijuana. Without this step, you are missing half of the compounds that will give you your desired effect.
Break up buds and place in an oven-safe dish. Bake at 220°F for 30-40 minutes, stirring every 10 minutes, or until the color changes and the moisture has evaporated. Do not leave unattended!
Don't want to use the oven? Try a decarb machine. Ardent makes a decarboxylator that will help you ensure accurate dosing and make sure you are getting all the benefits from your marijuana. See References for purchasing information.

Equipment Needs

Scale: Get a scale. No, not the tiny one that you use to measure out your nugs. Get a scale that will measure up to 5 pounds/2.2kg or, 11 pounds ideally. Your baking will be just that much more awesome when you can measure accurately. I promise.

A Standing Mixer is quite helpful for many of these recipes. Is it necessary? No. However, your time making recipes will increase, as you will be doing them all by hand. There are a few recipes that are difficult to make without one and those will be denoted as such. A majority of the time you will be using the paddle attachment.

What about a hand mixer? They work fine for some things, not so much for others. I'll note in the recipes if a hand mixer will work.

Thermometer: A thermo will help with making candies and custards. I recommend a digital probe thermometer. They usually run about $20 and are worth it. I also use mine when cooking meats, as you can run the probe line out of the oven and just set the temp. Genius.

Ice Cream Maker: The Cuisinart ICE-21 makes great ice cream! You keep the base in the freezer when not in use and it usually makes 1.5 quarts of ice cream in about 20 minutes. Other options include the ice cream soccer ball (SoftShell Ice Cream Ball) which is a hoot to play with, or even just a large freezer zip-close bag filled with ice and salt, a smaller zip-close sandwich bag filled with ice cream base and a few friends to help mash the bag around until it chills. See References for further directions on the zip-bag method.

Strainer: In professional kitchens, we call this a *chinois fine*. A strainer with a fine-mesh that is conical in shape will do nicely. Make sure you have cheesecloth on hand as well, it will take out the particulate matter, ensuring that your baked goods are not full of crunchy marijuana bits.

Cookie Scoop: Making evenly sized cookies is a snap with a spring-loaded scoop. All cookie recipes in this book have been tested with a #40 scoop, which yields 1.25 oz (35g) cookie dough lumps when packed tightly and leveled. Scoops, also called dishers, usually have the number stamped on the release slide in the bowl of the scoop, or on the handle.

Ovens: Every oven is different, especially home ovens. When I note a cooking time, check it 3-5 minutes *before* the done time to see how it is doing. Always rotate your products halfway through the baking time. No oven cooks evenly all the time.

A Note about the Measurements:

The recipes in this book are presented in Imperial Standard, home-baker style (cups and teaspoons, etc.). If you are more comfortable using recipes in weights, such as pounds and ounces or metric, please email me and I will send you recipes scaled appropriately. (Contact information is on the About page)

Converting Recipes to Gluten-Free, Vegan or Low-Sugar

M any of the recipes contained herein can be converted easily to Gluten-Free or Vegan. Whenever possible, I will note this in the Substitutions section.

Gluten-Free: I highly recommend King Arthur Flour's Gluten-Free Multi-Purpose Flour. It bakes up evenly and does not have that chalky taste and gritty mouthfeel that so many other GF flour blends do. I also like that you do not have to drastically increase the liquids in the recipes to compensate for the starches absorbing all the liquids.

Another great flour blend is Cup4Cup. Developed by Chef Thomas Keller, it is a wonderful blend that frees you from making a lot of adjustments in your recipes – just measure and go!

If you are interested in making your own flour blends, I recommend the book "Let Us All Eat Cake: Gluten-Free Recipes for Everyone's Favorite Cakes" by Catherine Ruehle and Sarah Scheffel. I have used the flour blends that are in the book numerous times with great results.

Remember that if you are baking for someone who is a Celiac patient, your kitchen needs to be 100% wheat flour free and that all your ingredients need to be certified Gluten-Free as well. Many Celiac patients I know are very sensitive and cross-contamination can make them very sick. Gluten is sneaky and hides in many condiments, including vanilla extract. Look at all the labels before using.

All recipes contained herein can be made using gluten-free flour blends without adjustment.

Vegan: Some recipes can be made Vegan in this book, others just will not (ice cream, I'm looking at you). You can substitute Cannabis Butter with Earth Balance vegan shortening or coconut fat. Use Ener-G Egg Replacer or make your own flax egg instead of chicken eggs. Substitute unsweetened plant milks (soy, almond, cashew, rice, etc.) for dairy milks when possible.

Make sure your sugars are vegan. Regular ol' cane sugar has been whitened using bone ash, so it is not appropriate for vegans. Sugar made from sugar beets has not been refined in that method, so it is safe to use. Gelatin can be replaced with agar agar, a refined seaweed that sets even when cold.

Egg Replacer vs. Flax Egg – when to use which product? Flax eggs work quite well in cookies and lower-moisture baked goods. Items that have a higher moisture content, such as carrot cake or zucchini bread, would work quite will with Egg Replacer, as the starches will gelatinize the excess moisture. Flax eggs are made by adding hot water to ground flaxseed and allowing the mixture to gelatinize, thus providing the binding job that chicken eggs do in non-vegan baked goods.

Low Sugar: The majority of my recipes are on the less-sweet side. I am not a fan of the super-sweet desserts. Some recipes have the ability for you to lower the sugar and replace with either applesauce or pearsauce. Keep in mind that some diabetics can tolerate fructose and others cannot. Many of the recipes in this book can have their sugar reduced by 10% safely without affecting the outcome. In baking chemistry, sugar acts as the tenderizer. Omitting sugar entirely will drastically change the texture of the baked goods.

Sucralose-based artificial sweeteners can be used, but again, caution is advised as some cannot tolerate it.

Cannabis Butter

Use in all recipes that call for butter, or heck, just enjoy on your morning toast.

Yield: 2lbs Cannabis Butter
Dosage: Approximately 23 milligrams (mg) THC per ounce
Time: 12.5 hours
Equipment:

- a large slow cooker, at least 6 quarts
- a fine-mesh strainer (chinois fine)
- cheesecloth
- large container to strain butter into

Ingredients:

- 2 lbs 4 oz butter, unsalted (9 sticks)
- ¼ oz (7g) high-potency marijuana (KB)

FIRST: Decarb your marijuana! Break up buds and place in an oven-safe dish. Bake at 220°F for 30-40 minutes, stirring every 10 minutes, or until the color changes and the moisture has evaporated.

Second: Unwrap butter and place all in slow cooker along with decarbed marijuana. Place slow cooker on Low setting with lid and let cook for 6 hours. Cook for an additional 6 hours on Warm. You want to have a low constant heat to pull the active THC out of the marijuana and into the butter.

This may stink up the house, but it's worth it.

Third: After 12 hours, strain butter through cheesecloth-lined strainer into a container. If butter still contains particulate matter, strain once more through fresh cheesecloth. Refrigerate butter until solid. Keep in fridge until ready to use, clearly labeled. Butter will keep in the fridge for up to 8 weeks.

<u>Non-Stinky Infusion Method:</u> Sous Vide machine! A sous vide (French for 'under vacuum') machine is a water heater and circulator. There are a few great sous vide machines for home use out on the market now and they've come down in price quite nicely; a good one will run you about $160.

<u>First:</u> Place your butter and decarbed marijuana into a pouch and heat seal (canning/mason jars work great too for smaller amounts).

<u>Second:</u> Place in a large container (a clean sink will work well) and fill with water. Set the sous vide to 85°C (185°F) and let circulate for four to six hours.

<u>Third:</u> Remove and let cool. When you can handle the pouches or jars and not burn the crap out of yourself, continue with straining, etc.

Vegan Variation: Use Earth Balance vegan shortening instead of dairy butter. Use caution, as it is more delicate than butter and can break down easily.

Cannabis Oil

Use in cooking food or in baked goods.

Deadly in marinara!

Yield: 1 quart (32 oz)

Dosage: Approximately 26 milligrams (mg) THC per ounce of oil

Time: 3 hours

Equipment:

- one large pan/stockpot or slow cooker
- cheesecloth
- fine-mesh strainer (chinois fine)
- funnel

Ingredients:

- 1 quart (32 oz) mild cooking oil, such as canola, vegetable or corn (reserve the container)
- 1/2 oz (14g) high-quality marijuana (KB), buds broken and decarbed

First: Hey! Decarb your marijuana! Break up buds and place in an oven-safe dish. Bake at 220°F for 30-40 minutes, stirring every 10 minutes, or until the color changes and the moisture has evaporated.

Second: In a large heavy-bottomed pan or double boiler (bain marie), place oil. Heat over low until you can smell the aroma of the oil. Add the decarbed marijuana buds and stir. Heat oil on low low heat for three hours, stirring occasionally. Do not allow oil to get very hot, or it will scorch the weed and make a mess in your kitchen. It will also make the oil taste terrible, and then you will be sad

Slow cooker method: Place oil and decarbed marijuana in a large 6-qt (5.67L) slow cooker. Place on Warm for three hours and stir occasionally.

Third: Remove from heat and allow to come completely to room temperature. Place several layers of cheesecloth into strainer and strain oil to another container. If there is a still particulate matter in your oil, strain again with fresh cheesecloth.

Use funnel and pour cooled, strained oil back into original container for ease of use. The oil can be stored at room temperature for a month, up to two months in the refrigerator. Label oil container appropriately.

Non-Stinky Method: See Sous Vide directions under Cannabis Butter.

Olive oil or Cannabis Oil? You decide.

Cannabis Coconut Fat

Coconut fat is a great way to include brain-healthy Medium Chain Fatty Trans Acids into your diet. Some recipes you can sub coconut fat for butter and convert the recipe to vegan. Or, just use some in your stir-fry. Yum.

Yield: 1 lb (16 oz) infused coconut fat

Dosage: Approximately 49 milligrams (mg) THC per ounce of coconut fat

Time: 4 hours

Equipment:
- one large pot, bowl that fits in the pot
- cheesecloth
- fine-mesh strainer (chinois fine)

Ingredients:
- 17oz (1 lb 1oz) Coconut oil (virgin is best)
- 1/4 oz (7g) high-quality marijuana (KB), buds broken and decarbed

The procedure for coconut is much the same as infusing vegetable oil. Due to the delicate nature of the fat, however, it is strongly recommended that you use a double boiler (bain marie).

First: Hey! Decarb!

Second: Place water in pot and put bowl on top. If water touches the bottom of the bowl, pour some out. Bring water to a boil. In bowl, place coconut fat and decarbed marijuana. Turn heat down to low and place bowl on pot. Allow fat to melt and infuse over lowest heat. Keep an eye on the water levels and do not allow your pot to cook dry.

<u>Third:</u> Remove from heat and allow to cool. Place several layers of cheesecloth into strainer and strain fat to another container. If there is still particulate matter in your fat, strain again with fresh cheesecloth.

Store labeled appropriately in the fridge for up to 8 weeks.

<u>Non-Stinky Method:</u> Follow directions under Cannabis Butter for sous vide. Circulate for four hours at 85°C (185°F).

Tinctures

Tinctures are alcohol-based infusions of marijuana. In many baking recipes, you can add a few drops to vanilla extract to bump up your treats. They're also great for people who want to medicate sublingually.

This recipe is strong and meant to be measured using a medicine dropper!

Yield: 4 oz marijuana-infused alcohol

Dosage: Approximately 420 (heh) milligrams (mg) per ounce of infused alcohol

Time: 30 minutes

Equipment:
- one small mason jar with lid and ring (8 oz jar)
- medium-size pot
- kitchen towel
- pair of tongs
- strainer
- cheesecloth
- medicine dropper, to dose final product

Ingredients:
- 4 oz (1/2 cup) high-proof alcohol (such as Everclear) see Variations, below
- 1/2 oz (14g) high-quality marijuana (KB), buds ground, decarbed

<u>First Step</u>: Decarb! (go ahead, I'll wait for you)

<u>Second:</u> Place decarbed marijuana in jar and cover with alcohol. Seal jar. Place kitchen towel in bottom of pot and place sealed jar on top. Cover jar with at least 1" of water. Over medium-low heat, simmer jar for 30 minutes.

<u>Third:</u> Use tongs to remove jar from hot water. Let cool to room temp and then strain. Label jar appropriately. Tincture will keep for months at room temp, tightly sealed. Some evaporation will occur over time, so use up your tincture within three months of creation.

Variations: Everclear is best, as it has no residual taste. However, it is not available in all states/provinces, so high-proof vodka is an option as well as brandy. Brandy (cheap VSOP) will add a flavor, so is acceptable in baked goods, but may not be great if you're cooking savory items with it.

Giddyup!

J ust so you know -- **All** of the following recipes will work with regular ol' unsalted butter, vegetable oil, coconut fat, etc. Infused Edibles are great, but what if you need a regular (unleaded) cake or to bring something to a BBQ and you need a great recipe?

I gotchu!

Everything is super tasty, and you will be the hero of your outing. Promise.

Chocolate Chippers

veryone needs a great chocolate chip cookie recipe that isn't off the back of the bag. This is that recipe.

Yield: 40 cookies

Dosage: Approximately 5mg THC each cookie

Time: 1 hour

Equipment:

- standing mixer (optional)
- spatula
- measuring cups
- measuring spoons
- cookie sheets
- parchment paper
- spring-loaded scoop, size #40
- cooling rack

Oven: Preheat oven to 350°F

Ingredients:
- 8 oz (1 cup) Cannabis Butter, room temp
- ¾ cup sugar
- ¾ cup brown sugar
- 2 eggs
- 1 ½ tsp vanilla extract
- 2 1/4 cups all-purpose flour
- ¼ tsp salt
- 1 ½ tsp baking soda
- 2 ½ cups semi-sweet chocolate chips

In a medium bowl, combine all dry ingredients (flour, salt, baking soda) and set aside.

Pool together eggs and vanilla extract in a small container.

Place butter and both sugars in mixing bowl. Mix together on low speed until sugars are completely incorporated and butter is a bit fluffy. Add in eggs and vanilla extract and mix until completely combined. Stop your mixer periodically and use spatula to remove dough from paddle attachment.

Add dry ingredients and mix until about ¾ of the way combined. There will be flour still not mixed in (but that's ok!). Add chocolate chips and mix until all the way combined (no dry bits showing!). Do not over mix! We want delicious cookies, not hockey pucks. I will sometimes stop the mixer, scrape the paddle and finish mixing the dough by hand to make sure that I don't have any stray butter chunks.

If cookies are not mixed properly, when baked you will have high, tight and puffy cookies and sad flat cookies all in the same batch.

Use spring-loaded scoop and scoop cookies onto baking sheets lined with parchment paper.

Bake @ 350°F for 12 minutes, turning sheets halfway through.

Vegan Variation: Replace Cannabis Butter with Cannabis-infused Earth Balance. Use flax eggs or Egg Replacer.

These are not terrible.

Chocolate Crinkles

Can't decide if you want a brownie or if you're in a cookie mood? This is both worlds in one, in other words, A Perfect Cookie. These are Super Sneaky – it is hard to tell that there is marijuana in these. When you want an Edible with not a lot of marijuana flavor, this is for you.

Yield: 36 cookies
Dosage: Approximately 3mg THC per serving
Time: 1 hour
Equipment:
- standing mixer (optional)
- spatula
- measuring cups
- measuring spoons
- small & medium bowls
- sifter or sieve
- cookie sheets
- parchment paper
- spring-loaded scoop, size #40
- cooling rack

Oven: Preheat oven to 325°F

Ingredients:
- 4oz (1/2 cup) Cannabis Oil
- 2 cups sugar
- 4 eggs
- 2 tsp vanilla extract
- 2 cups all-purpose flour
- 2 tsp baking powder
- ½ tsp salt
- 1 cup unsweetened cocoa powder
- powdered sugar to roll cookies in, approx. 1 cup

In a medium bowl, sift together all dry ingredients. Cocoa clumps and does not mix in well if it has not been sifted.

Pool your eggs and vanilla in a small container.

In mixing bowl, combine sugar and vegetable oil and mix until sugar is completely coated with the oil. Add eggs, one at a time, making sure that it is incorporated before adding the next. Fold in remaining dry ingredients into the batter.

Fridge batter for 30 minutes, up to an hour. This allows time for the batter to firm up and gives the flour a chance to start absorbing all the liquids in this recipe.

Scoop using spring-loaded cookie scoop and roll in powdered sugar until heavily coated. Place on baking sheets lined with parchment and bake @ 325°F for 10-12 minutes, turning halfway through. These cookies are best when underbaked a bit, so check at the earlier time for doneness.

Vegan Variation: Use Egg Replacer instead of chicken eggs.

OMG YAS.

Snickerdoodles

This is the first cookie I ever learned how to bake. It's my dad's favorite, although he prefers the Unleaded version. If your Cannabis Butter has a lot of chlorophyll, these cookies will have a green tinge to them.

Yield: 36 cookies

Dosage: Approximately 5mg THC per cookie

Time: 1 hour

Equipment:
- standing mixer (optional)
- spatula
- measuring cups
- measuring spoons
- cookie sheets
- parchment paper
- spring-loaded scoop, size #40
- cooling rack

Oven: Preheat Oven to 350°F

Ingredients:

- 8oz (1 cup) Cannabis Butter
- 1 ½ cups sugar
- 2 eggs
- 2 tsp vanilla extract
- 2 ¾ cups all-purpose flour
- 2 tsp cream of tartar
- 1 tsp baking soda
- ¼ tsp salt

<u>To roll cookies in:</u>

- ¼ cup sugar
- 1 tbsp cinnamon, ground

In a medium bowl, combine all dry ingredients (flour, baking soda, cream of tartar and salt) and reserve.

Pool your eggs and vanilla extract in a small container.

In a mixing bowl cream butter and sugar together until light and fluffy. Scrape the bowl and paddle attachment. Add eggs and vanilla, mix until thoroughly combined. Scrape. Add drys and mix until just combined.

Use cookie scoop, scoop into balls and roll in cinnamon/sugar mix until heavily coated. Place on parchment-lined cookie sheets and bake @ 350 for 12 minutes, turning sheets halfway through, until cookies are lightly browned and set in the middle. Let cool and enjoy!

Vegan Variation: Use Cannabis-infused Earth Balance instead of Cannabis Butter. Use Egg Replacer or flax egg instead of eggs.

Molasses Spice Cookies aka "Little Brown Cookies"

On a camping trip, these were labeled "Little Brown Cookies" and the name has stuck ever since then. The spices in these pair nicely with the herbaceous flavor of marijuana, masking it just a bit. Even without Cannabis Butter, these are simply the best cookie around.

Yield: 28 cookies

Dosage: Approximately 5mg THC per cookie

Time: 45 minutes

Equipment:

- standing mixer (optional)
- spatula
- small and medium bowls
- measuring cups
- measuring spoons
- cookie sheets
- parchment paper
- spring-loaded scoop, size #40
- cooling rack

Oven: Preheat Oven to 350°F

Ingredients:

- 6 oz (3/4 cup) Cannabis Butter
- 1 tsp ginger, ground
- ¼ tsp clove, ground
- 1 tsp cinnamon, ground
- 1 cup brown sugar, packed
- 1 egg
- ¼ cup molasses
- 2 cups all-purpose flour
- 2 tsp baking soda
- ¼ tsp salt
- 1 cup Sugar in the Raw or turbinado sugar, for rolling

In a medium bowl, place dry ingredients (flour, baking soda, salt) and reserve.

Pan-spray a liquid measuring cup and measure out molasses. Place egg on top.

Cream butter, sugar and spices together until well combined and fluffy. Add egg and molasses, mixing until incorporated. Scrape bowl and paddle. Add dry ingredients and mix until just combined. Use spatula to ensure dough is homogenous.

Scoop and roll in coarse sugar (Sugar in the Raw or turbinado). If you can't find either sugars, plain white sugar will work as well. Your cookies won't have quite the texture of the raw sugar, but they'll still be delicious.

Place on parchment-lined cookie sheets and bake @ 350°F for 10-12 minutes, turning halfway through, or until cookies have set in the middle. Remove from tray and let cool, try to not eat them all in one sitting (ha!).

Vegan Variation: Use Cannabis-infused Earth Balance instead of Cannabis Butter. Replace egg with flax egg.

Pretty much the best cookie ever.

ANZAC Biscuits

If you're not Australian or a New Zealander, you may not know what these tasty biscuits are: a perfect combination of orange, oats, coconut and honey. Traditionally, they are made without orange, but I think they're fantastic with it. These come together in a snap and are irresistible. Orange blossom water can be obtained from a Middle Eastern or Indian grocery, or your best friend, Amazon.

Yield: 20 cookies
Dosage: Approximately 5mg THC per cookie
Time: 45 minutes
Equipment:

- a large mixing bowl,
- medium mixing bowl
- small saucepan
- spatula
- measuring cups
- measuring spoons
- a rasp or grater such as a Microplane
- cookie sheets
- parchment paper
- spring-loaded scoop, size #40
- cooling rack

Oven: Preheat Oven to 325°F

Ingredients:

- 1 cup all-purpose flour
- 1 cup rolled oats
- ½ cup sugar
- ½ cup brown sugar, packed
- 1 cup shredded unsweetened coconut
- ½ tsp salt
- 4 oz (1/2 cup) Cannabis Butter
- 2 Tbsp Lyle's Golden Syrup or honey (orange blossom honey is great)
- zest of one medium orange
- 1 tbsp boiling water
- ½ tsp baking soda
- 2 tsp orange blossom water

In the large mixing bowl, place all the dry ingredients (flour, sugars, oats, coconut, salt) and mix thoroughly.

Zest orange, being careful to take only the top layer and not the white pith, and place in small saucepan with butter and honey. Melt butter mixture over low heat until completely melted. Do not allow to boil.

In a small container, place baking soda and pour boiling water over. Stir to combine and dissolve baking soda. Pour baking soda solution into melted butter, making sure that you have scraped alllll the baking soda out of the container. Add orange blossom water and stir.

Pour liquids into bowl containing drys (flour, coconut, etc.) and mix very well until no dry bits are present. I sometimes dig in with my paws to make sure that it's all evenly mixed.

Scoop onto parchment-lined baking sheets and flatten a little. Don't leave in mounds, as they will not spread like other cookies and the middles will be weird and doughy.

Bake 11 – 13 minutes @ 325°F, turning baking sheets halfway through, until deeply golden. Let cool. These cookies are a nice combination of crisp and a bit chewy.

Vegan Variation: Replace Cannabis Butter with Cannabis-infused Earth Balance or Coconut Fat. Increase flour to 1 ¼ cups.

Maybe just a *bit* too close together . . .

Peanut Butter Oatmeal

At one time, I was the pastry chef for a large hotel chain. I made these regularly as Amenities (treats for VIPs) as well as bribe material for our Head Engineer so he would fix things in the kitchen for us. It always worked.

If you want to gild the lily, as they say, add 10 oz (2 cups) mini chocolate chips as the last step.

Yield: 44 cookies
Dosage: Approximately 5mg THC per cookie
Time: 45 minutes
Equipment:
- standing mixer (optional)
- spatula
- measuring cups
- measuring spoons
- cookie sheets
- parchment paper
- spring-loaded scoop, size #40
- cooling rack

Oven: Preheat Oven to 350°F

Ingredients:
- 8 oz (1 cup) Cannabis Butter
- 1 cup brown sugar, packed
- ¾ cup sugar
- 1 cup peanut butter, creamy
- 2 eggs
- 2 cups All-purpose flour
- 2 tsp baking soda
- 1 tsp salt
- 1 cup rolled oats

In a bowl, combine all dry ingredients (flour, baking soda, oats, salt) and set aside.

Pool your eggs in a small container and reserve.

Combine butter and both sugars in mixer and beat until fluffy. Add peanut butter and mix until completely incorporated. Add eggs and mix. Scrape your bowl and paddle attachment.

Add dry ingredients and mix until just combined. Scrape bowl and paddle, ensuring all is evenly mixed.

Scoop onto parchment-lined cookie sheets and press down slightly to flatten. Bake @ 350°F for 12-14 minutes, turning baking sheets halfway through. Let cool.

Vegan Variation: Substitute Cannabis-infused Earth Balance in place of Cannabis Butter. Use flax egg in place of eggs. If you use natural peanut butter, increase sugar to 1 ¼ cups.

Hello, Lovers!

Sour Cream Brownies

These are my favorite brownies ever. Super easy, super versatile. Additional flavor ideas can be found after the main recipe. These are also deadly, as you can hardly taste the marijuana in them.

Yield: one 9"x 13" pan, 12 brownies
Dosage: Approximately 23mg THC per brownie
Time: 1 hour
Equipment:
- one large mixing bowl
- medium saucepan
- whisk
- spatula
- measuring spoons
- measuring cups

Oven: Preheat oven to 350°F

Ingredients:
- 12 oz (1 ½ cups) Cannabis Butter
- 1 cup unsweetened cocoa powder
- 4 eggs
- 2 ½ cups sugar
- 1 Tbsp vanilla extract
- 2/3 cup full-fat sour cream
- 1 cup all-purpose flour
- ½ tsp salt

Line baking pan with aluminum foil, leaving enough over the sides to form a sling so you can easily remove the brownies once baked. Pan spray the inside of the pan.

Pool eggs in small container and reserve.

Combine flour and salt in small bowl and reserve.

Melt butter in saucepan over low heat. Remove from heat and whisk in cocoa, set aside and let cool.

In a large bowl, place sugar and eggs. Whisk vigorously until eggs lighten in color. Stir in cooled butter/cocoa mixture and vanilla extract. Whisk in sour cream until combined. Using spatula, fold in flour and salt until combined – no dry bits!

Pour into prepared pan and bake @ 350°F for 35-40 minutes, turning pan halfway through baking, or until toothpick inserted in middle of brownie comes out mostly clean.

Let cool and then portion. Don't leave this as one giant brownie Pangea – it is super easy to overdose on this one!

Variations:
Chocolate Orange: add grated zest of one orange to butter and melt together. Proceed with recipe as above.

Chocolate Mint: add 1 tsp mint extract to batter along with vanilla extract. If using mint oil, start with a few drops and taste a tiny amount of batter when it's all combined. If it needs more, add more. Remember that mint can get toothpaste-y rather quickly, so it's advised to start with a lower amount.

Aztec Hot Chocolate: Add 1 tbsp ground cinnamon, 1 tsp ground allspice and ¼ tsp cayenne pepper to butter and proceed with remainder of recipe.

Earl Grey Brownies: Cut open three Earl Grey teabags and add to butter. Melt butter and steep tea for 20 minutes off heat. Strain out tea solids before whisking in cocoa.

Double Chocolate: Fold in one 10 oz bag dark chocolate bittersweet chips into batter just before baking. Sinful.

Vegan Variation: Substitute Cannabis-infused Earth Balance for the Cannabis Butter. Use Egg Replacer for the chicken eggs and your favorite vegan sour cream for the dairy sour cream. Increase flour to 1¼ cups, as the vegan sour cream has a higher moisture content.

BRB, gonna shove this in my face

Chocolate Caramel Shortbread Bars

H oly cannoli – these are amazing! There is a bit more work to these, but they are so, so worth it. Make these when you want to Treat Yo Self.

Note: you will need 3g of decarbed marijuana in addition to the Cannabis Butter needed for the shortbread base.

Yield: one 9 inch square pan, 24 bars
Dosage: Approximately 19mg THC per bar
Time: 1 hour 15 minutes plus 3 hours cooling time
Equipment: two medium saucepans
- two small bowls (heatproof)
- whisk
- rubber spatula
- liquid measuring cup
- ladle
- measuring cups
- measuring spoons
- thermometer

Oven: Preheat to 350°F

Ingredients:

*Caramel Sauce:

- 1 ½ cups sugar
- ¼ cup water
- 1 ½ cups (12 fl oz) heavy whipping cream

*Shortbread Base:

- 4 oz (1/2 cup) Cannabis Butter
- 1/3 cup brown sugar
- ½ tsp vanilla extract
- ¼ tsp salt
- 1 cup all-purpose flour

*Chocolate Caramel Filling:

- 8 oz (1 cup) heavy whipping cream
- 3g high-potency marijuana (KB), decarbed
- 8 oz (1 cup) caramel sauce
- 4 large egg yolks
- 5 oz dark chocolate, 60% or higher**
- flake sea salt, for finishing (Maldon is great)

This recipe has three components: **caramel sauce**, **shortbread crust** and **chocolate caramel filling**. Caramel sauce is made first as it is a component in the filling, then shortbread crust and finally the delicious chocolate caramel filling. The bars are then assembled and let to cool.

Make the **caramel sauce** first. Place water in 2 qt heavy-bottomed saucepan and then add sugar. Use high heat and cook until sugar is a deep amber in color. Do not stir! Don't walk away! Once color is achieved, turn off heat and add cream slowly. This will bubble and boil like lava, so please be careful. Nothing hurts like a sugar burn!

Once caramel has stopped bubbling, put back on low heat, whisking until there are no hard sugar lumps in the caramel sauce. Remove from heat and allow to come to room temperature. Once cool, taste the caramel sauce and make sure it is pleasantly caramelly in taste and not burnt and awful. This recipe makes more than what you need for the chocolate caramel filling, so reserve the remainder for your ice cream or morning coffee. Yum.

Chocolate Caramel Filling, Step One: Place decarbed marijuana in saucepot with 8 oz heavy cream. Allow cream to come to a simmer (not boil). Turn off heat and cover, steeping for 30 minutes.

While your cream is steeping, make the **shortbread crust**. Line your pan with aluminum foil, allowing for an overhang so you can remove the bars from the pan easily once they are set. Pan spray the foil.

Cream together Cannabis Butter and brown sugar. Add vanilla. Add in salt and flour and mix until just combined. This should be a soft dough.

Spread dough evenly in baking pan, making sure it reaches up the sides at least an inch. Dock (prick) dough all over using tines of a fork. Freeze dough for 20 minutes and then bake.

Bake until golden, about 15-18 minutes. Allow crust to cool.

Chocolate Caramel Filling, Step Two: While crust is cooling, separate your eggs. Reserve whites for another use.

Place yolks in a small bowl. Put strained infused cream and 8 oz (1 cup) caramel sauce in a saucepot and bring to a simmer over medium heat.

Using a ladle, temper hot cream mix into yolks, streaming in a little at a time and whisking. Return cream and yolks to pan, cooking over medium-low heat and stirring with spatula constantly until mixture coats the back of a spoon, or reaches 170°F (*a la nappé*) on your probe thermometer.

Pour hot caramel mixture directly on to chocolate. Allow to set for 30 seconds and then stir with spatula, moving from the inside of the bowl to the outside. Do not use a whisk at this point, as it will allow too much air into the mixture.

Pour mixture into waiting crust and allow to set up. Fridge for 3 hours uncovered or until completely set. Bars will keep for about a week tightly wrapped in the fridge.

For serving: Cut into squares and dust each piece with the sea salt. Don't skip this step, as it totally makes these bars swoon-worthy.

**Look at the packaging on your chocolate. Percentage indicates how much chocolate liquor is in the mix. Milk chocolate is low, usually 38%, white chocolate is 0% and good dark chocolate 58% or higher. The higher the percentage, the more bitter the taste, as it has less sugar. For this recipe, I like 63% as it complements the marijuana taste and brings out the caramel notes.

Variation: Use pre-made tart shells instead of making your own shortbread crust. This will cut down on the dosage, but if you're pressed for time, it's a good shortcut.

Vegan Variation: I've tried several substitutes and I was not super satisfied with the results. So, you're on your own for this one, my little vegan kittens.

So. Good.

Banana Bread

There are few things better in life than having your house fill with the heavenly aroma of baking banana bread. This recipe makes a super tender and moist loaf – perfect for Banana Bread French Toast or just enjoying slathered with butter.

Yield: one 9"x5" loaf pan, about 8 slices. 2 lbs 10 oz batter per pan -or- 18 muffins

Dosage: Approximately 13mg THC per slice, 6mg THC per muffin

Time: one hour plus cooling time

Equipment:
- two medium size bowls
- one small bowl
- whisk
- rubber spatula
- measuring cups
- measuring spoons
- liquid measuring cup

Oven: 350°F

Ingredients:
- 2 eggs
- 1/3 cup liquid buttermilk
- ½ tsp vanilla extract
- ¼ tsp almond extract, optional
- 4 oz (1/2 cup) Cannabis Oil
- 1 cup or 3 each bananas, very ripe
- 1 ½ cup sugar
- 1 ¾ cup all-purpose flour
- 1 tsp baking soda
- ½ tsp salt
- ½ tsp cinnamon
- *Optional*: ½ cup nuts, toasted

Line loaf pan with foil, using enough to create an overhang. Pan spray foil in pan and set aside.

Mush up the bananas in a small bowl and set aside.

Place sugar, flour, baking soda, salt and cinnamon in a bowl and whisk all dry ingredients together.

In a medium bowl, whisk eggs, buttermilk, extracts and oil together.

Add wet ingredients into drys. Add bananas and fold until completely combined.

Pour into prepared pan and bake at 350F for about 60-75 minutes. There is a lot of moisture in this recipe, so it may take longer to bake completely. Bread is done when a skewer or toothpick is inserted in the middle and comes out clean, no crumbs. Allow to cool before slicing.

Variation: Awww nuts! Some people really love nuts in their B-Bread, others don't. Personally, I really love this topped with Sugar in the Raw and natural sliced almonds before baking. I've tried it with walnuts, pecans, almonds and sesame seeds all with great results. However, you do you.

Muffin variation: Make Banana Bread and scoop batter into muffin tin prepared with liners or pan-sprayed. Fill each tin 2/3 full and bake about 35 – 45 min or until toothpick inserted in center comes out clean.

Vegan Variation: Replace buttermilk with vegan buttermilk: 1 tbsp acid to 1 cup of non-dairy milk (e.g. 1 tbsp lemon juice and 1 cup (8oz) soy milk). Use Egg Replacer for chicken eggs.

Glorious.

Zucchini Bread

In the part of the country where I live, zucchini grow to be the size of cricket bats and usually take over the garden. One neighborhood I lived in was famous for the ding-dong-ditch lady who would leave grocery sacks piled high with zucchini on your front porch and run. This zucchini bread is a great way to use up those that grow tough and woody.

Yield: two 8"x4" pans, 1 lb 13 oz batter each pan (12 slices total) – or 18 muffins

Dosage: Approximately 17 mg THC per slice, 24mg THC per muffin

Time: one hour

Equipment:
- two medium sized bowls
- one small bowl
- box grater
- paring knife
- whisk
- rubber spatula
- measuring cups
- measuring spoons

Oven: 350°F

Ingredients:
- 3 eggs
- 8 oz (1 cup) Cannabis Oil
- 1 tbsp vanilla extract
- 2 cups zucchini, grated, about 2 medium size, 14 oz total
- 2 ¼ cups sugar
- 3 cups all-purpose flour
- 1 tsp salt
- 1 tsp baking soda
- 1 tsp baking powder
- 1 tbsp cinnamon
- optional: 1 cup nuts, toasted
- optional: one 10 oz bag mini chocolate chips

Prepare your pans. Either foil or line with parchment and pan spray. Set aside.

Wash up your zucchini. Using a paring knife, lop off stem and blossom ends. Do not peel. Grate on a box grater using the largest holes, or if you've a food processor, use that. Reserve.

In a bowl, place flour, salt, baking soda, baking powder and cinnamon. Whisk to combine.

In another bowl, whisk eggs, oil, vanilla and sugar together. Stir in zucchini.

Pour all wets into drys and fold together using rubber spatula until completely combined.

Bake at 350F for 35-40 minutes for 9"x13" pan or 50-65 minutes for loaf pans.

Bread is done when a skewer or toothpick inserted in the middle comes out clean, no crumbs or batter clinging to the toothpick.

Variations: Again, we're having The Nut Discussion. This is your bread, you make it how you like. It's great naked, it's great with walnuts or pecans. It is really great with mini chocolate chips folded into the batter just before baking. So. Pick your poison.

Muffin variation: Make Zucchini Bread and scoop batter into muffin tin prepared with liners or pan-sprayed. Fill each tin 2/3 full and bake about 30 – 40 min or until toothpick inserted in center comes out clean.

Vegan Variation: Use Egg Replacer instead of chicken eggs.

The raw sugar crust on top totally makes this amazeballs.

Pumpkin Bread

am one of those people who feel that pumpkin is acceptable any time of year, not just in the fall. This bread is moist and full of pumpkin spice goodness that scratches an itch you didn't even know you had.

Note: Pumpkin typically comes in 15 oz cans.

This recipe is one that you must bust out your scale for, as the pumpkin and Cannabis Oil need to be weighed.

Yield: one 9"x5" loaf pan, eight slices, 2 lbs 9oz batter total
Dosage: Approximately 17mg THC per serving
Time: 1 hour 45 minutes
Equipment:
- standing mixer or hand mixer
- one small bowl
- one medium bowl
- measuring spoons
- measuring cups
- whisk
- rubber spatula

Oven: 350°F

Ingredients:

- ¼ cup plus 1 cup sugar
- 3 egg whites (3 oz), reserve yolks for another use
- 13.25 oz canned pumpkin
- 5.25 oz Cannabis Oil
- 1 tsp ginger, ground
- ½ tsp nutmeg, ground
- 1 ½ tsp cinnamon, ground
- ¾ tsp allspice, ground
- ½ tsp cloves, ground
- ¾ tsp salt
- ¾ tsp baking soda
- 1 ½ tsp baking powder
- 2 cups all-purpose flour

Line loaf pan with aluminum foil and pan spray. Reserve.

This recipe incorporates a simple meringue (egg whites and sugar) into the batter to lighten the texture of the finished bread.

In the bowl of a standing mixer, place egg whites. Using whip attachment, mix on low speed until whites break up and start to look foamy. Crank up the mixer to medium and slowly add in ¼ cup sugar while it is mixing. You are making a simple meringue. If you add all the sugar in at once, the meringue will never whip up and it will be sad. Continue whipping once all sugar is added in until meringue reaches stiff peaks. When you pull the whip off the machine, the whites will stand at a peak and not be soft, oozy or droop. If it's still soft, put back in the machine and whip until stiff peaks are achieved.

In a small bowl whisk pumpkin and oil together. Reserve.

Place all dry ingredients into medium bowl including 1 cup sugar. Reserve.

Add pumpkin oil mix to dry ingredients and combine. Mixture will be stiff.

Take a third of your meringue and mix into pumpkin vigorously with your spatula. Take another third and fold gently into mixture, thinking happy thoughts about how awesome this bread is going to be. Continue with remaining meringue and fold until there are no streaks.

Pour into prepared pan and bake for 55 - 65 minutes. Bread is done when a toothpick inserted into middle comes out clean.

Vegan Variation: Add sugar into drys. Make Egg Replacer and add to pumpkin and oil mixture. Pour wets into drys, fold until completely combined and pour into loaf pan and bake. Loaf will be more dense, but still delicious.

Measuring. Makes you strong like bull . . .

Sour Cream Coffee Cake or Muffin Base

There are times when you need coffee cake to accompany your morning coffee or tea. This versatile recipe can be coffee cake or muffins, both of which freeze beautifully, allowing you to meal prep your medicated breakfast like a boss.

Yield: 9"x9" square pan, eight pieces, or 12 muffins
Dosage: Approximately 23mg THC per serving, 15mg THC per muffin
Time: one hour
Equipment:
- a standing mixer or hand mixer
- 3 small bowls
- rubber spatula
- measuring cups
- measuring spoons

Oven: Preheat oven to 350°F

Ingredients:
- 1 cup (8 oz) Cannabis Butter
- 1 ½ cups sugar
- 3 eggs
- 1 egg yolk
- 1 ½ tsp vanilla extract
- 1 cup (8 oz) sour cream
- 2 ½ cups all-purpose flour
- 2 ½ tsp baking powder
- ¼ tsp salt

*Streusel topping:
- ¼ cup (2 oz) Cannabis Butter
- ½ cup brown sugar, packed
- ½ cup all-purpose flour
- ½ cup rolled oats
- ½ tsp cinnamon
- pinch of salt
- pinch of black pepper

*Muffin Fruit:
- 1 pint fresh blueberries or 1 cup frozen
- zest of one lemon

This is a stiff batter, so using a machine (stand mixer, hand mixer) is your best bet. If you're Popeye or augmenting your CrossFit workout, do this by hand.

For Coffee Cake: Prepare pan by lining with parchment, making sure you have overhang, so you can lift the coffee cake out with ease when done. Pan spray parchment and reserve.

In a medium bowl, combine dry ingredients (flour, baking powder, salt) and reserve.

Pool eggs, yolk and vanilla extract together in a small container and reserve.

Place butter and sugar in mixing bowl and mix on low speed until completely incorporated. Add eggs, yolk and vanilla, mixing on low until combined. Scrape the bowl and mix again on low until there are no butter chunks and batter is homogenous. Add sour cream and mix. Add remainder of dry ingredients and mix until combined. Be sure to scrape bowl to ensure complete incorporation.

In a small bowl, place all streusel ingredients. Rub butter in until completely integrated.

Place batter in pan and lay streusel mix evenly over top, lightly patting to adhere to batter.

Bake for 55 – 65 minutes or until toothpick inserted in center comes out clean.

Muffins: Line a 12-muffin tin with liners or pan spray.

Combine dry ingredients in a small bowl. In another bowl, place frozen blueberries and 2 tbsp of dry mixture, turning to coat (omit this step if you are using fresh, as they will not sink as much in the batter).

Place butter, sugar and lemon zest in mixing bowl and mix on low speed until completely incorporated. Add eggs, yolk and vanilla, mixing on low until combined. Scrape the bowl and mix again on low until there are no butter chunks and batter is homogenous. Add sour cream and mix. Add remainder of dry ingredients and mix until combined. Add berries tossed in flour and mix gently on low to incorporate. If you mix on too high of a speed, the berries will disintegrate, and you will have purple muffins. Be sure to scrape bowl to ensure complete incorporation.

Scoop into muffin tin, 2/3 full. Top with streusel or Sugar in the Raw. Bake for 25 – 35 minutes or until toothpick inserted comes out clean.

Fruit Variations: Sky's the limit on this! Blackberry with a zested orange is glorious. So is raspberry with white chocolate chips. Strawberry is lovely too. Pick your fave and go for it.

Vegan Variation: Substitute vegan sour cream for dairy sour cream and use egg replacer for the chicken eggs. Increase flour to 2 ¾ cups.

Coffee + a slab of this streuseled wonder = best. Breakfast. Ever.

Gingerbread

This is definitely something you'll want to pull out for the Holiday Season this winter. A slab of this will take the edge off Mom and calm down your crazy uncle. You might even survive your family with this seasonal cake . . .

Yield: one 9"x13" pan, 12 portions
Dosage: Approximately 8mg THC per portion
Time: 45 minutes
Equipment:
- standing mixer or hand mixer
- small saucepan
- small bowls
- whisk
- measuring cups
- measuring spoons
- liquid measuring cup
- rubber spatula

Oven: 350°F

Ingredients:

- ½ cup (4 oz) Cannabis Butter
- 1 cup (8 fl oz) molasses
- 2 eggs
- 1 cup brown sugar
- 2 cups AP flour
- 1 tbsp+ 1 tsp cinnamon, ground
- 1 tbsp + 1 tsp ginger, ground
- ½ tsp ground cloves
- ½ tsp salt
- 2 tsp baking soda
- 1 cup (8 fl oz) boiling water
- 1 cup orange marmalade (8 oz jar)
- 1 cup finely chopped pecans or walnuts (optional)

Prepare pan: line with parchment, ensuring overhang so you can remove cake easily and pan spray. This cake is *sticky!*

Pan spray your liquid measuring cup and measure in molasses.

Heat butter and molasses over low heat until melted and stir to combine. Let cool.

In mixer using paddle attachment, beat eggs and brown sugar well, until eggs are lighter in color. Pour in butter/molasses and beat until well combined.

With mixer on low, fold in dry ingredients until just blended. Combine baking soda and boiling water. Whisk in marmalade. Pour into batter and gently mix. Add nuts (if using) and stir until just combined.

Turn out batter into pan and bake in oven for 30 – 40 minutes, or until toothpick inserted in the middle comes clean.

Let cool and flip out of pan while still slightly warm. Remove parchment and serve with whipped cream or dusted with powdered sugar.

Vegan Variation: Substitute eggs with Egg Replacer. Use Cannabis-infused Earth Balance instead of butter. Increase flour to 2 ¼ cups.

Lemon Pound Cake

I will freely admit to loving lemon more than chocolate, a view my spouse does not share. This pound cake is dense and intensely lemony. If lemon is not your jam, check out the variations listed at the end of the recipe.

This recipe is adapted from Chef Sherry Yard's amazing cookbook, "The Secrets of Baking".

Yield: one 9"x5" loaf pan, eight slices
Dosage: Approximately 23mg THC per slice
Time: one hour and 45 minutes
Equipment:

- a standing mixer or hand mixer
- liquid measuring cup
- a zester or rasp, such as a Microplane
- citrus reamer/juicer (optional)
- measuring cups
- measuring spoons
- rubber spatula
- two small bowls
- one larger bowl
- sifter or strainer
- wooden skewer

Oven: 350°F

Ingredients:
- 1 cup (8 oz) Cannabis Butter
- 1 cup sugar
- 2 tbsp grated lemon zest
- 2 eggs
- ¾ cup all-purpose flour
- ¾ cup cake flour
- ½ tsp baking powder
- 1/8 tsp salt
- ½ cup (4 oz) liquid buttermilk
- 1 tbsp fresh lemon juice

*syrup for basting
- ½ cup (4 oz) lemon juice
- ¾ cup sugar
- 1 tbsp lemon zest

*flat icing (optional)
- 1 cup powdered sugar (icing sugar)
- ¼ cup lemon/citrus juice

This cake is best with fresh lemon juice. The concentrated stuff in the green bottle will not cut it here.

Prepare your loaf pan by lining with parchment paper and pan spraying. Set aside.

This pound cake uses the modified creaming method, meaning that we cream the butter and sugar together and add in dry ingredients alternating with the liquids.

In a liquid measuring cup, measure out buttermilk and add lemon juice. Reserve.

Measure out all dry ingredients and use sifter or strainer to sift into larger bowl. Cake flour clumps easily due to the high starch content and the lumps don't get worked out by the mixer. No one likes lumpy cake.

Pool eggs in small container and reserve.

In the bowl of your mixer, place the sugar, butter and lemon zest. Mix together well until completely incorporated.

Add eggs and mix, scraping after adding each egg.

Add ½ flour mix and start mixing on slow. Stream in ½ of the buttermilk/lemon.

Add remainder of flour and again, while mixing on slow, stream in buttermilk/lemon. Mix until completely incorporated, scraping often.

Pour batter into loaf pan and bake for 70-80 minutes. A toothpick inserted in the middle comes out clean when this is done.

While the cake is baking, make your syrup. Place lemon juice, zest and sugar in a small saucepan. Bring to a boil and cook for about 3 minutes, or until sugar has dissolve. Reserve.

When cake comes out of the oven, immediately use wooden skewer to poke a bunch of holes in the cake. Those of you rockin' the Jell-O poke cake know this technique.

After your pound cake is nice and holey, gently pour warm syrup slowly over the cake, allowing the hot cake to absorb the syrup.

Cake should be completely cool before cutting into portions.

Variations: Not crazy about the syrup? Make a flat icing by whisking lemon juice into powdered sugar and ice the cake while still warm.

Lime: substitute lime for lemon.

Lemon-Lime: This is my favorite. Use 1 tbsp lemon zest and 1 tbsp lime zest for the cake. Keep the lemon juice in the buttermilk but use lime juice for the soaking syrup.

Grapefruit-Vanilla: Use grapefruit instead of lemon. Scrape the seeds from a vanilla pod and add to the sugar/butter creaming step. Add 2 tsp vanilla extract in with the eggs.

<u>Lime-Coconut:</u> Replace lemon with lime and add ½ cup toasted sweetened coconut into the drys. Make syrup with unsweetened coconut milk (3 oz) and lime juice (1 oz), reduce sugar to ½ cup.

<u>Lemon Poppyseed:</u> Remove 2 tbsp of flour from recipe. Add 2 tbsp poppyseed to buttermilk mixture and allow to stand for 20 minutes before using.

Vegan Variation: Replace buttermilk with vegan buttermilk: 1 tbsp acid to 1 cup of non-dairy milk (e.g. 1 tbsp lemon juice and 1 cup (8oz) soy milk). Use Egg Replacer for chicken eggs. Replace butter with Cannabis-infused Earth Balance.

Cream Scone

This is a pretty great way to start your day. Make these the night before for the perfect medicated breakfast or put the *high* in High Tea.

Yield: eight scones
Dosage: Approximately 45mg THC per scone
Time: one hour
Equipment:
- medium-sized bowl
- small saucepan
- strainer
- measuring cups
- measuring spoons
- whisk
- rubber spatula
- bench knife (or chef's knife)
- pastry brush
- baking sheet and parchment

Oven: 350°F

Ingredients:
- 1 ¼ cups (10 fl oz) heavy whipping cream
- 3g high-potency marijuana (KB), decarbed
- 2 cups all-purpose flour
- 1 tbsp baking powder
- ½ tsp salt
- ¼ cup sugar
- flavoring: berries, fruits, nuts, etc. See Variations.
- 2 tbsp heavy cream for topping
- Sugar in the Raw for topping

Place cream and decarbed marijuana in a small saucepan. Bring up to a simmer and then turn off heat. Steep marijuana in cream for 20 minutes. Strain and reserve. This step can be done a day in advance, if desired.

Place remainder of ingredients in a bowl and whisk together. Also add in flavorings (see below for options).

Pour infused strained cream into bowl. Using a rubber spatula, fold cream into dry ingredients, making sure to work the cream in entirely. No dry bits! If your scone dough is really dry, add in a tbsp of cream.

Throw a little flour down on the counter. Plop the scone dough out of the bowl and pat into an 8" round circle. Use the bench knife to help keep the sides nice. Using bench knife (or chef's knife), cut into 8 equal pie pieces.

Place triangles of dough on parchment-lined baking sheet. Using reserved 2 tbsp of cream, brush onto tops of scone triangles and sprinkle with Sugar in the Raw.

Bake for 20-30 minutes or until scones are light brown and set.

Flavor Variations: This recipe adapts to a lot of different flavors, so have fun!

Apple Cinnamon: Add two apples (granny smith or other hardy apple), peeled and diced along with 1 tsp cinnamon and ¼ tsp ground ginger to drys.

Banana Almond: slice up two ripe bananas and add ½ cup sliced almonds to the drys.

Blackberry Orange: zest and suprème (cut off rind and cut out orange sections in between membranes) one orange and add ½ pint fresh blackberries (halved if they are large) to the drys.

Blueberry Lemon: add ½ pint fresh blueberries and the zest of half a lemon to the drys.

Ginger Peach: Add two fresh peaches diced, along with 1 oz (three good chunks) crystallized ginger, minced, to drys.

Pear Cardamom: add two ripe pears, peeled and diced along with 1 tsp ground cardamom to drys.

Raspberry Chocolate: add ½ pint fresh raspberries and ½ cup mini chocolate chips to the drys.

Spice: add 1 tsp cinnamon, ½ tsp allspice, 1 tsp ginger, 1/8 tsp cloves and 1/8 tsp ground black pepper to drys.

Strawberry: add ½ container strawberries, hulled and sliced to drys.

Vegan Variation: Infuse Cannabis in soy milk or nut milk instead of cream.

Blackberry Orange, you have my heart.

Melty Mints

If you love mint and chocolate, this will light your fire (in the best way possible, of course). This is adapted from Chef Peter Greweling's comprehensive book about confections, "Chocolates and Confections: Formula, Theory and Technique for the Artisan Confectioner".

Note: break out the scale for this one – you must weigh everything.

Yield: 64 one-inch by one-inch (1" x 1") pieces
Dosage: Approximately 3mg THC per piece
Time: 45 minutes
Equipment:
- medium saucepan
- one medium bowl
- spatula
- chef's knife
- ruler
- cutting board

Oven: no oven needed!

Ingredients:
- 3 – 5 drops peppermint oil (or ½ tsp mint extract)
- 3.6 oz Cannabis Coconut Fat
- 12.3 oz dark chocolate, 58% or higher, cut into small chunks if in bar form
- 1 cup powdered sugar, for coating

Line an 8" x 8" square pan with aluminum foil and set aside for later.

Place water in pot and put bowl on top. If water touches the bottom of the bowl, pour some out. Bring water to a boil.

In bowl, place dark chocolate and Cannabis Coconut Fat. Set on pot of barely simmering water and melt, stirring often. Do not walk away!

Once chocolate has 80% melted, remove from heat and stir until the residual heat has melted the rest of the chocolate. Add mint extract or peppermint oil. Take a tiny taste to see what your level of mint is. Once again, be cautious with the mint. If it needs more, add small amounts until it tastes the way you want it.

Pour out mixture into pan and refrigerate until firm, about 20-30 minutes. You want to be able to remove the slab in one piece, but you don't want it to be completely set and hard, as that will make it super difficult to cut. The texture will be like a softened chocolate bar (think s'mores: the chocolate bar when it melts a little after being in contact with your lightly charred marshmallow).

Once it is set enough to handle, turn chocolate slab out on a cutting board. Use your chef's knife and ruler, cut into 1" x 1" pieces and place in powdered sugar to coat.

Store confections packed in the powdered sugar in a tightly sealed container in the fridge, labeled appropriately. Mints will last about three weeks.

Savory Breakfast Biscuits

Many mornings, I would make these for breakfast to feed my poor starving culinary students. They are killer with a fried egg, making them world's best breakfast sandwiches.

You can sub in different kinds of meat or make them meat-free.

Yield: 12 biscuits
Dosage: Approximately 8mg THC per biscuit
Time: 30 minutes
Equipment: large bowl
- smaller bowl
- liquid measuring cup
- measuring cups
- measuring spoons
- rubber spatula
- large spring-loaded scoop (#8)
- baking sheets
- parchment

Oven: 350°F

Ingredients:
- 2 ¼ cups all-purpose flour
- 1 tsp sugar
- ½ tsp baking soda
- 1 ½ tsp baking powder
- 1 ½ tsp salt
- ½ tsp ground black pepper
- ¼ tsp cayenne pepper
- ½ cup (4 oz) Cannabis Butter
- ¼ cup chopped mixed herbs/onions (see below for variations)
- ½ cup grated cheese (see below for variations)
- ½ cup chopped meat (optional)(see below for variations)
- 1 egg
- 1 cup (8 fl oz) liquid buttermilk

In a large bowl, place all dry ingredients. Using your fingers, rub butter into drys until completely absorbed.

Add in cheese, herbs and meat (if using) and toss to combine.

Whisk egg and buttermilk together. Add into bowl and using spatula, stir to combine.

Use large scoop (#8) or, if you don't have one, use a ¼ cup dry measure to make biscuit mounds and place onto baking sheets lined with parchment.

Bake for 20-30 minutes, or until biscuits are golden brown.

Variations: Breakfast-y type meats work great here. Chopped bacon, ham or cooked sausage are all winners.

Cheeses: sharp cheddar, asiago, swiss, gruyere, pepper jack, etc.

Herb Mix: I usually start with 2 tbsp chopped fresh parsley and add in a member of the onion family. Scallions (green onion or spring onion), shallots, onion or sautéed leeks are all great.

<u>Combos:</u>
- Sharp cheddar, ham, fresh rosemary and shallot.
- Gruyere, bacon, leek
- Marble Jack, scallion, bacon
- Monterey Jack, sausage, scallion
- *Student Favorite*: Extra cheddar and scallion, no meat

Vegan Variation: Use Egg Replacer, Cannabis-infused Earth Balance and vegan buttermilk. Omit cheese (soy cheeses do not melt well in this application) and add in extra veg such as cooked chopped broccoli florets, diced bell pepper, diced portobello mushrooms, etc.

Breakfast of Champions.

Ice Cream

omemade ice cream is an exponential level above anything store-bought, and this particular recipe is really quite special. The base recipe comes from an insanely creative and talented pastry chef I had the fortune to work under, LM.

For many medical marijuana patients, especially those undergoing chemo, this is the easiest and best way to medicate. See Milkshake variation below.

This recipe takes about three days due to cooling and steeping, but it is 110% worth it.

While you cannot copyright recipes, the procedures and directions contained herein are copyright Pastry Princess Enterprises LLC.

Yield: 2 quarts (64 oz)
Dosage: Approximately 15mg THC per 1 oz scoop
Time: three days (don't freak – it's worth it)
Equipment:
- large bowl
- large saucepan
- medium bowl
- liquid measure
- measuring spoons
- rubber spatula
- thermometer
- whisk
- ladle
- strainer
- cheesecloth
- large container to strain into

- ice cream maker
- pint containers (paper or plastic)

Ingredients:
- ¼ ounce (7g) high-potency marijuana (KB), decarbed
- 5 cups (40 fl oz) heavy cream, 38% fat content or higher
- 2 cups (16 fl oz) whole milk
- 1½ cups sugar, divided
- 1 tsp salt
- 4 eggs
- Flavorings (see variations below)

This ice cream uses a method called Cold Infuse. You are going to be infusing the marijuana and flavorings for 24 hours before making the custard. Some flavorings are added in Day One, some in Day Two after the custard is made.

Add-ins, also known as inclusions, are to be added once the ice cream has been churned and before it is packed into containers. Place your churned ice cream in a large very cold bowl (fresh out of the freezer) and use a spatula to mix in your inclusions (nuts, marshmallows, pretzels, mini chocolate chips, etc.). You do not add them in while churning, as the machine will beat up the inclusions and make your ice cream have a terrible texture as well as possibly breaking the machine (it can ruin the motor).

Day One: In a large pan, place cream and milk, half the sugar, decarbed marijuana and whole flavorings. Bring up to a simmer. Pull off heat and allow to cool. Do not strain! Once cool, cover and put in the refrigerator for 24 hours.

Infuse, my pretty!

Day Two: Pull cream infusion out of fridge. Grab your large container and place strainer lined with cheesecloth over the opening. Set aside.

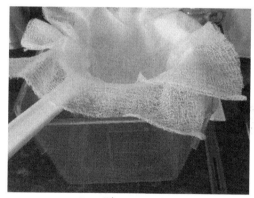

Et voilá, ze container

In a medium bowl, place eggs, salt and other half of sugar. Whisk immediately. Do not allow eggs and sugar to sit without whisking, as the sugar will "cook" the eggs, prematurely coagulating them and inhibit the binding of the custard later.

Bring cream mixture to a simmer once again. Using a ladle, add hot cream into egg mixture in a steady stream while whisking. Use 1/3 of the hot cream to temper into the yolks. If you just dump in the hot cream without adjusting the temperature of the eggs (temper), you will curdle and coagulate the eggs and ruin your custard.

Once you have a third of the hot cream in the egg business, put the tempered eggs into the pot with the hot cream.

Cook over medium-low heat, stirring constantly with rubber until mixture coats the back of a spoon, or reaches 170°F (*a la nappé*).

Immediately pull off heat and strain into waiting container. Do not allow custard to sit, as it will continue to cook in the pan and you will end up with scrambled marijuana eggs instead of ice cream custard base. At this point, some of the flavorings will be added in while the custard is still hot.

Place custard in the refrigerator <u>uncovered</u> and allow to cool. Once custard has cooled to 40F or lower, you can cover the container. Allow custard to sit overnight.

Day Three: Pull out your ice cream maker machine and frozen insert. Add in dasher. Take custard out of the fridge and whisk before churning, as it will have separated somewhat overnight.

Fill machine according to manufacturer's instructions. Most home-style ice cream makers will make 1 ½ pints per churning session. I can usually coax two runs out of my frozen insert before it gets too warm.

Churn custard for 20 -30 minutes or until custard appears like soft-serve ice cream. Do not over churn! If your ice cream is over-churned, it will be hard and grainy, having separated the milkfat from the custard. It will taste ok, but the texture will be terrible, and you will be sad.

Stop machine and pull out dasher. Use spatula and remove ice cream. Pull ice cream out of machine and into a large frozen bowl. If you are using inclusions, add them in at this stage, using a spatula to mix into your frozen custard.

Pack into containers, label and date. The "freezer canning" plastic containers work great for this if you can't get your hands on the paper containers.

Churn baby churn!

How to Fix Your Ice Cream if You've Effed it up:

If on Day Two, while making your custard, you've overcooked it --how do you fix it?

- strain through sieve, no cheesecloth. This is merely to sift out the marijuana buds.
- Using an immersion blender (or regular blender), blend on high speed until custard is smooth, no lumps or chunks.
- Strain custard through sieve lined with layers of cheesecloth.
- Taste to ensure that texture is smooth, and custard is not burnt.
- Chill custard

This works about 80% of the time. If you've really scalded it, your custard will taste terrible, and there is no recovery from that, sadly.

Milkshake: Take two scoops ice cream and place in blender or immersion blender container. Add whole milk until it covers the scoops and blend until smooth. Enjoy. This is a particularly good way to medicate if you or someone you love has been going through chemo, as it is easy to eat and feels good going down.

Berry:
- 1 lb berries, cooked, pureéd and strained (no seeds please!)
- ½ vanilla bean, split
  - Place vanilla bean in with cream and milk on Day One.
  - Add berries to hot strained custard on Day Three. Whisk to combine and then cool.

Chai:
- 3 black tea bags, cut open
- 1 vanilla bean
- 1 piece star anise
- 2 tsp whole cardamom, crushed
- 2" piece fresh ginger, sliced
- 1 tsp whole black peppercorns
- 1 tsp whole allspice berries
- 2 whole cinnamon stick

  Place all flavorings in with cream and milk in Day One.

Chocolate:
- 12 oz dark chocolate, 58% or higher

  Place dark chocolate in the bottom of your large container in Day Three. Strain the hot custard into the container. The heat will melt the chocolate. Whisk to combine and then cool.

Coffee:
- ½ cup dark roast coffee beans, crushed
- 1 vanilla bean

  Place coffee and split vanilla bean in cream and milk in Day One.

Dreamsicle:
- zest of two oranges
- two vanilla beans
- 2 tsp vanilla extract

  Add flavorings to cream and milk in Day One, add extract to finished custard on Day Three.

<u>French Vanilla:</u>
- three vanilla beans
- 3 egg yolks
  Add vanilla beans, split and scraped, to cream and milk in Day One. Add additional yolks to eggs in Day Two.

<u>Honey Thyme:</u>
- 4 sprigs fresh thyme or 2 tsp dried thyme
- one half vanilla bean pod
- 8 oz honey
- reduce sugar to ¾ cup
  Place thyme and half vanilla bean in with cream and milk on Day One. Add honey in with eggs on Day Two.

<u>Mint Chocolate:</u>
- 12 oz dark chocolate, 58% or higher
- mint extract, to taste -or- Peppermint Oil (7 drops)
- 10 oz mini chocolate chips (optional)
  Place dark chocolate in the bottom of your large container in Day Three. Strain the hot custard into the container. The heat will melt the chocolate. Whisk to combine. Add mint extract, ¼ tsp at a time, tasting after each addition. You want pleasantly minty, not chocolate toothpaste.
  Use mini chocolate chips as an inclusion on Day Three.

Creamy Mint Chocolate Chip goodness.

Mocha:
- 10 oz dark chocolate, 58% or higher
- ½ cup dark roast coffee beans, crushed
- half a vanilla bean

  Place coffee beans and vanilla in cream and milk in Day One.

  Place dark chocolate in the bottom of your large container in Day Three. Strain the hot custard into the container. The heat will melt the chocolate. Whisk to combine and then cool.

Rocky Road:
- 12oz dark chocolate, 58% or higher
- mini marshmallows
- pretzel rods
- salted peanuts

  Place dark chocolate in the bottom of your large container in Day Three. Strain the hot custard into the container. The heat will melt the chocolate. Whisk to combine and then cool.

  Add mini marshmallows, pretzels and nuts on Day Three as inclusions.

Salted Caramel:
- 1 ½ cups caramel sauce
- sea salt to taste

  Add salted caramel to hot custard in Day Three. Whisk to combine. Taste and adjust with sea salt. It should taste salty, but not briney.

References

Decarboxylator Machine:
"Buy NOVA Decarboxylator - US Usage." *Ardent Cannabis*, Ardent Cannabis, LLC, ardentcannabis.com/products/nova-decarboxylator/.

High Altitude Baking:
"A Complete Guide to High Altitude Baking." Edited by Patricia Kendall, *CSU Extension*, csuextstore.com/a-complete-guide-to-high-altitude-baking.

King Arthur Flour Company, Inc. "High-Altitude Baking." *King Arthur Flour - Try It Once, Trust It Always*, King Arthur Flour, www.kingarthurflour.com/learn/high-altitude-baking.html.

Make Ice Cream in a Bag:
Goldfield, Hannah. "A Master's Twist on Making Ice Cream in a Plastic Bag." *The New Yorker*, The New Yorker, 11 July 2018, www.newyorker.com/culture/kitchen-notes/a-masters-twist-on-making-ice-cream-in-a-plastic-bag.

THC Dosage Calculator:
Sicard, Cheri. "U.S. THC or CBD Dosage Calculator." *Cannabis Cheri: Marijuana Recipes, Lifestyle, Activism and Entertainment*, www.cannabischeri.com/cannademy-dosage-calculator/.

Books:

Greweling, Peter P. *Chocolates and Confections: Formula, Theory, and Technique for the Artisan Confectioner*. Wiley, 2013.

Ruehle, Catherine, et al. *Let Us All Eat Cake: Gluten-Free Recipes for Everyone's Favorite Cakes*. Ten Speed Press, 2014.

Yard, Sherry. *The Secrets of Baking: Simple Techniques for Sophisticated Desserts*. Houghton Mifflin, 2003.

Acknowledgements

This would not have been possible without the love, nagging and support from my Spouse, my rock.

Special thanks to JM and ME for supplies.

To my taste testers: DM and JK, SW and DM, JH and DP, LS and KS, MB, AC & ZC, TW & DL thank you all so much for your time and feedback.

Extra love to my editor, SAH

To my Homeslice Sistars who keep me real: EAO, DM and SW, MB and SAH.

Big love to LM for the ice cream recipe.

To my former students: thanks for being amazingly awesome people. You know who you are.

Finally, to everyone who's heard me talk about this for the last three years (or more!) ad nauseum, thanks for putting up with me.

About

S. Jackson, *aka* The Pastry Princess is a pastry chef, educator and consultant and is ACF accredited. She currently lives in a state that recognizes medical marijuana, but not recreational and has been a chef for the last 15 years.

Stints in just about every kind of kitchen there is along with being a chef instructor for the next generation of chefs has given her a wide breadth of experience that she is here to share with you.

Her favorite thing to bake is cookies because they make everyone happy.

Stay in touch!

www.incredible420edibles.com

Email: pastryprincessbakes@gmail.com
Instagram: incredible420edible
Facebook: https://www.facebook.com/Incredible420Edibles/
Twitter: www.twitter.com/420CWPC

14038471R00058

Made in the USA
Lexington, KY
04 November 2018